CW00867360

'Devotions to the *only* 3 in 1 - a 40 day devotional'

By Ruth Chambers, Debbie Jones, Lucy Ncube, Sharon Davis & Doreen Joseph

Photographs from Carol Bourne, Mercedes Powe, Alithea, Safron & Doreen Joseph

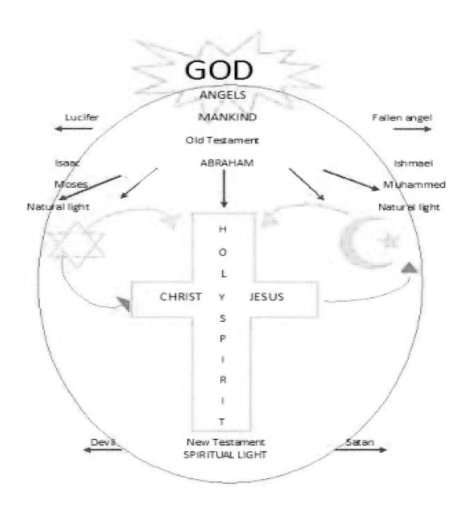

Father, Son & Holy Spirit - (Perfect Circles relationships with mankind)
Printed by Kindle Direct Publishing (KDP.COM)
Independently Published London (2023)
ISBN: 9798389262287

Sisters in Christ....His devotees,

Doreen Joseph, Ruth Chambers, Sharon Davis, Debbie Jones & Lucy Ncube

Photoshot, Mercedes Powe

Devotions to the only 3 in 1 - a 40 day devotional

CONTENTS PAGES:

CONTENTS contd.

Grace and Encouragement

Advice / Admonition

Special Prayers

Epilogue

Our Acknowledgements:

Ruth's Acknowledgements

My Heavenly Father, He truly is my everything. I thank Him for this opportunity, the joy I have experienced in being used by Him. I thank Him for the will and ability to engage in this project and see it through to the end. I owe it all to Him.

I couldn't ask for a better daughter - Mercedes, my precious gift from God and my son-in-law Nicholas, his undoubted kindness has not gone unnoticed. They have been my biggest support system every step of the way.

My sincerest gratitude to my four sisters in Christ, Doreen, Debbie, Carol and Lucy. It has been an honour and privilege to collaborate with you on this project. I am inspired by your love for God, your determination and zeal to do His will.

A special thank you to Doreen for spearheading the project and for her guidance and invaluable support.

Doreen's Acknowledgements

'Give praise and thanksgiving for Father Yahweh's uncounted mercies and countless blessings that He gives us daily - every single day! (Holy Spirit inspired 2016 when Yahweh blessed us with a fabulous once in a lifetime, 4 generational family reunion in Grenada, W. I.)

Praises and thanks also are due to Lord Jesus Christ, our co-Creator, REDEEMER and Saviour for His wondrous selfless voluntary life-giving and life-saving sacrifice on Calvary's cross, and His resurrection that gives us hope of eternal life in Perfect Circles relationships with Them.

Thanks to the Holy Spirit for inspiring and guiding us through this project and our lives.

Gratitude to the wonderful ladies and prayer warriors - Ruth, Debbie, Lucy, Carol and Sharon, who collaborated with me on these devotions. I'm truly humbled and delighted by them. It's been a special time and privilege to serve the Lord in this way with them. May Yahweh reward and sustain them exceedingly and abundantly (Ephesians 3 v 20).

I'm grateful to my daughters Alithea, and Safron who provided photos of flowers from Kenya and Kew Gardens, and Carol's garden flowers in W. London, my photos from Grenada, Shrigley hall & hotel, Macclesfied, Manchester and Isleworth flowers; & Mercedes' photoshots; supplemented by Shutterstock; and free internet images. Thanks also to my 'adopted' daughter Natalie L. Mark for helping with film info and support.

My sincere prayer is that you are blessed and touched by the depth and strength of our devotions of love and adoration for heavenly Father Yahweh and Jesus Christ, that you too will experience such.

Debbie's Acknowledgments

I would like to thank God who is my enabler. Without Him I would not be able to achieve this outcome. I give Him thanks.

I would like to thank my husband Adrian for his encouragement and faith in me. And for my children: Jonathan and his wife Lucy with little Noah, Joanna, Joel and Tamara, twins Judith and Julia, and our adopted son Seth and his wife Patience and their son Adrian, who helped me to believe in myself.

Finally, I would like to thank Doreen Joseph for inspiring me to write. She has been pushing me for many years.

Lucy's Acknowledgements

My first and foremost acknowledgement is to the Most High God, Jesus Christ and Holy Spirit whom I could never imagine being without. Secondly I am grateful to the women of God whom I have had pleasure to work with in this project.
We met monthly for over a year to discuss and encourage each other from a blank canvas to now. May the good LORD richly bless you all, as we lift up the name of Jesus Christ.
Finally, but not least, I acknowledge my family who are a blessing and continue to be by my side.Once again thank you all for this privilege.

Sharon's acknowledgements

I would like to thank Papa for placing people in my life to encourage, inspire and help me become the woman our Heavenly Father is molding me to be.

Thanks to my children, Michaela, Kevron, Ramone, Seth, Jude, Grandson Noah and son-in-law Chris. Joanne, Doreen, Delsie, Laura, Edith, Delores, Joy and Sis Rainbow, Carol. Women of God who look out for me and call my name in prayer, more times than I dear count. Thank you for holding me up in your prayers my Sisters in Christ.

God bless all the people in my life. As every encounter, good or otherwise, He has used for His glory. Amen.   (iii)

Carol's mix pot, London

(iv)

Our Introductions:-

Doreen Joseph's intro

So Christmas 2021, my daughters and I were standing at the entrance of Shrigley Hall Hotel & Spa, Macclesfield, surveying its beautiful expansive grounds. Then the thought came into my mind, 'wouldn't this picturesque natural scenery be perfect for a book to inspire tranquility, peace of mind, even ecotherapy?' as someone for whom through nature, our Creator, heavenly Father Yahweh, brings healing and mental well-being. The scene was set, the seed sown, but better yet, it could be a collaboration from our SDA church sisters/friends who loved the Lord with deep devotion; a few of whom had recently participated in Angus Buchanan's 21 day online daily devotion. I invited the women here, who immediately agreed, and our project was born.

Taking a line from a film 'life is like a box of chocolates, you never know what you're gonna get' (Forrest Gump, 1994) - our book is a collection of devotions from each of our personal perspectives and life experiences, with our unique personalities, yet united in love for our Creator, Redeemer and Saviour, Jesus the Christ, and His and our heavenly Father Yahweh. Originally titled 5 women and a photographer - 40 day devotional, it morphed into 49 days, then 50 day devotional. This was to reflect the Jewish Jubilee - 49/50th sabbatical year, where slaves/ servants were freed, debts were canceled, and possessions lost or forfeited were restored. Due to unforeseen circumstances we had changes to our line up, and reverted to a 40 day devotional.

Finally, on sabbath morning, 11/3/23, I dreamt the title name change to 'Devotions to the *only* 3 in 1 - a 40 day devotional'. Upon its completion we would celebrate our achievement; which in itself points to Christ' celebration at His 'marriage feast with His bride - the saved, elect, saints in heaven in the future, (Revelation 19 v 6 - 9; Ephesians 5 v 22 - 32). In the year of our book's preparation, Queen Elizabeth II celebrated her Platinum (75 years) Jubilee,(2022) before her death a few months later.

Notwithstanding, we, writers, celebrate our Holy Spirit inspired, devout adoration and appreciation of the Lord, and our gratitude for the lives He's given us, from which we can share and encourage others, especially through most difficult times. It wasn't smoothe or without obstacles.

Christ's arch enemy, the devil, tried to hinder our progress by health and financial challenges. However, we serve an Almighty Father Who fought our battles, (2 Samuel 22 & psalm 18) delivered us from painful physical, mental and emotional valleys, and cupped us in His righteous right hand (Isaiah 41 v 10 - 13) of loving care and protection. To cap it all, the book captures His beautiful creations in pictures - flowers and natural wonders, and art, depicting Yahweh's loving 'Perfect Circle relationships.'
We hope you are blessed and encouraged by it.

Ruth Chambers' Intro

God's Word, my journey throughout life, has taught me that life without God is without hope and meaning. I thank God for lovingly and tenderly bringing me to this spiritual point in my life. I thank Him for the ultimate sacrifice that He paid for my life. Because of God I have life, so I choose to live my life for Him. I am a vessel to be used by God, for His will. I am a vessel to be used by God for this project. My prayer is that souls will be brought to Christ through this 40-days devotional book. Truly God gets the glory.

May God bless you
Ruth M. Chambers

Debbie's Intro

When I was asked to contribute to this book by Doreen Joseph, I thought it a privilege and an honour. Writing my own book has been something I dreamed of doing, but I've been procrastinating for some years now.

My reason for wanting to write is to share scripture thoughts, to help others to understand scriptures, and to make them aware that scriptures can be a daily builder to boost their relationship with God and also with their fellow human beings.

Scripture reading also encourages wiser mind thoughts and better coping skills. Understanding scriptures also gives a hope for a better life to come with Jesus.

Part of my daily prayer is that God will make me to be an example through my life and through the words I write to be a true testimonial of Him.
I pray that as you read this book God will come alongside you to empower you by the renewing of your mind. God is always willing and ready to reveal Himself to anyone who comes searching for Him.

Lucy's intro

All things work together for those who love God and are called for His purpose. Romans 8:28.

I have always known that God has a plan and purpose for my life. However if anyone asked me to write my thoughts up to a year ago I would have told them

it is impossible. My interest began years ago reading Bible Verse of the Day and reading other believers' devotionals. I started sharing these scriptures on Social media and eventually became convinced to share my faith thoughts and beliefs. God opened a door when I joined up with like minded women of God in this project.
The rest is history.
My prayer is that you will be encouraged by these devotionals. For we serve a mighty God.

Sharon's intro

Sharon got baptised at Balham SDA Church; because she wanted to give her daughter the best thing she received in life, that her Grandparents Sylvia and Prudent Davis introduced to her, "Jesus!"

Sharon believes in the Bible and the promise that our Heavenly Father says to her in Joel 2:
 I will restore the years the canker and palmer worms have eaten. I will give you double for all your sorrow.

God is my Restorer.

With much love, may you be blessed as you read these devotions.

Lily pond Kew Gardens by Safron

(ix)

The *only* 3 in 1:- Father, Son & Holy Spirit

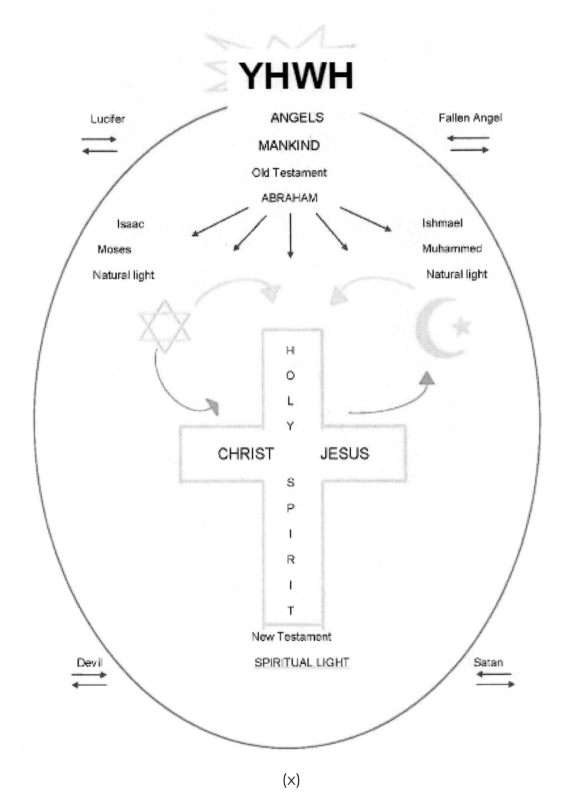

(x)

Alpha & Omega

(Shutterstock.com)

1. "I AM that I AM"
(Acknowledgement)

'God' told Moses that His name is YHWH (Yahweh), meaning 'I AM That/ Who I AM' (Exodus 3 v 14 - 15). He was and is the God of the Israelites, His chosen people. In fact, He said, "I AM the God of your fathers, the God of Abraham, the God of Isaac, and the God of Jacob." "YHWH" "is My name forever, and this is My memorial unto all generations."

Elsewhere He affirms that "I AM He: I AM the First and I AM the Last. My hand laid the foundation of the earth," (Isaiah 48 v 12 - 13).

He and Jesus Christ are One and the same, (John 10 v 32): -
"I and the Father are One." Indeed, They both say:
I AM Alpha and Omega, the First and the Last, the Beginning and the End, the Author and Finisher / Perfector of our faith" (John 1 v 1 - 5; Rev. 1 v 4 - 8; & Rev. 22 v 13; Hebrews 12 v 1 -2; & E G White, 'The Acts of the Apostles', chp. 30 (1845/1970); & EGW. 'The Story of Redemption' chp. 37, p273 (1947/1980); & D. Joseph, 'Perfect Circles ... vol. 1' chp. 9, p262-263).

Furthermore, because of Them and the (7) Holy Spirits (Rev. 4 v 5) we have our very existence! To us They are Father and Brother, Lord and King, Creator, Provider, Protector, Redeemer and Saviour for any and all of us who acknowledge, thank, follow and worship Them.

PRAISES: To Them be all laud, honour, power, praises, thanksgiving and glory forever and ever, amen.

Doreen Joseph (4th & 19th June '22).

(Shutterstock.com)

2. Put God First
(God first)

Matthew 10:37 (KJV) He that loveth father or mother more than me is not worthy of me: and he that loveth son or daughter more than me is not worthy of me.

To put God first is to love God with all our heart, soul and mind and to intrinsically allow God's word to become the authority over our lives; our thoughts, words and actions. In essence, it is full surrender and submission to His will. It also means, we put no one or nothing before God. Thus, it's often alarming when those who proclaim their love for God defend their spouse, children, family, friend when their words or behaviours are contrary to the word of God.

God continuously calls us to put Him first. To be His light bearers, in a world where it's becoming increasingly challenging to uphold God's righteousness. Popular values, theories and opinions are often in conflict with the word of God. However, we are called as soldiers in the army of the living God to bear the cross of Christ and when we do, rest assured, God will not leave us defenseless. He will surround us with His spirit and strengthen us with His divine power (Isaiah 41:10).

(to be continued...)

Kew Gardens, London, by Safron

Be encouraged dear friends, put God and His word first and foremost. Let us not get caught up in the profane and vain babblings of this world (2 Timothy 2:16). Stand up for God's righteousness so we will be worthy of Him (Matthew 10:37) and hear the words "Come, ye blessed of my Father, inherit the kingdom prepared for you from the foundation of the world" (Matt. 25:34). Put God first!

My Prayer - Dear Heavenly Father, thank You for Your word which is our authority and guide to righteousness. Please give us the desire and will to love You with all our hearts and to put You and Your word first. As we continually strive to uphold righteousness, we will face challenges from many people including family and friends. However, help us to always remember that our full surrender and submission should be to You only. Help us to gain strength from Your promises, to never leave or forsake us; You will always be with us to comfort, cheer and strengthen us. We thank You. We love You. In Jesus' name, I pray amen.

Ruth M. Chambers (April 2022)

(Shutterstock.com)

3. LOVE
(Grace)

"For God so loved the world that He gave His only begotten Son, that whosoever believeth in Him should not perish, but have everlasting life. For God sent not his Son into the world to condemn the world, but that the world through Him might be saved" (John 3:16,17). "To the praise of the glory of His grace, by which He made us accepted in the beloved". (Ephesians 1:6,7).

It can be difficult at times to understand God's love and grace towards us. When we talk about love, we are looking at love as being emotions and affection. Grace on the other hand is a favour or a gift often given spontaneously. God's grace is free and unmerited.

He bestows on sinners His grace because of His love for mankind. Grace is given to man, not that we deserve it. It is an undeserved favour of God's love for us. We can say that God's love and grace are connected as they go together like our text tells us: "God so loved the world that He gave His Son". And His grace works effectively to change our hearts to love as He loves, and as He cares. God's grace and love leads to Salvation.

For God so loved the world that He "gave His son". What a compassionate and loving, thoughtful and caring Father!

PRAYER

O Father, today I place my confidence in Your word and I cast all my cares upon You, because You cared so much for me that You sent Your only Son to save me. You are a thoughtful and caring Father. I return my thanks to You.

Amen.

Debbie Jones (Feb. 22).

(Shutterstock.com)

(SDA hymnal song 195 'Showers of blessings',

by Daniel W. Whittle (1840 - 1901) & James McGranahan (1840 - 1915)
Review & Herald Pub. Assocn. USA, 1985)

Worship, Praise & Thanksgiving

Prayer 15

I love You, Lord,
Singing 'I love You, Lord...'
Singing 'I love You, Lord...'
Ohhh! I love You!

(copyright IN MOMENTS LIKE THESE I SING OUT A SONG - GRAHAM DAVID (c) 1980 C.A. Music/Music Services Administered by Song Solutions www.songsolution.org)

(from Doreen's book 'Prayers for a child')

4. Praise God
(Praises)

Psalm 34:1 (KJV) I will bless the Lord at all times, His praise shall continually be in my mouth.

With a grateful and thankful heart, I praise God from whom all blessings flow (Ephesians 1:3).

I praise God for blessing us with His Love. For God so loved the world, that he gave his only begotten Son, that whosoever believeth in him should not perish, but have everlasting life (John 3:16).

I praise God for blessing us with His kindness. Every good and perfect gift comes from God (James 1:17).

I praise God for blessing us with His compassion. A woman may forget her sucking child, that she should not have compassion, yet God has promised that He will not forget us (Isaiah 49:15).

I praise God for blessing us with His mercy. God's mercies never fail, they are new every morning (Lamentations 3:22-23).

I praise God for blessing us with His grace. For by His grace are we all saved (Acts 15:11).

I praise God for blessing us with His patience. God is patient (Romans 15:5), slow to anger, gracious, kind and merciful (Jonah 4:2).

I praise God for blessing us with His forgiveness. Through His begotten Son, we have redemption and forgiveness of our sins (Colossians 1:14).

I praise God for blessing us with His faithfulness. God's faithfulness is great, it will never fail (Lamentations 3:23 & Psalm 89:33).

(to be continued...)

(Soweto women choir; google.com)

I will never get tired of praising God because He never gets tired of blessing me with His love, kindness, compassion, mercy, grace, patience, forgiveness and faithfulness. With a grateful and thankful heart, God I praise You.

Prayer – Dear Father in Heaven, I thank You and Praise You for all Your blessings. I thank You in a special way for Your begotten son, through which we can have salvation and eternal life. I pray that Your praise will forever be in my mouth because of who You are and all that You have done for us. We love You and praise You from whom all our blessings flow in Jesus' name amen.

Ruth M. Chambers (July 2022)

'I will bless the LORD at all times;
His praise shall continually be in my mouth.'
Psalm 34 v 1

(Etsy)

5. The Power of Praise and Worship
(Praise & Worship)

The Psalmist in Psalms 34:1 declares " I will bless the LORD at all times, His praises shall always be in my mouth "

This was not to say everything was always going well for David. In fact it was the opposite and David knew the power of praise. It is in those times when things don't seem to be moving, we are in spiritual warfare, our children seem to have lost their way, when the bills pile up, when we cannot feed our kids, when the mortgage is not paid, when we lose our jobs and our prayers seem to be going nowhere, when there's silence, that praise produces results so much faster even as we begin singing.

We are created to worship our Heavenly Father even when our hearts are heavy, because there's always something to praise Him for. Sometimes we can behave like a chicken as soon as it finishes eating it still rubs its beak on the ground as if to say "You didn't feed me, I am hungry." We also do the same as we forget about yesterday's blessings and start grumbling.

If we could develop a heart of praise no matter what we are going through we will see the power of our praises. I have seen it with my eyes and I can testify that God listens and hears our voices of praise and worship.
Man sometimes only sings praises when everything is going well and forgets that God is the same yesterday, today and forever.

Habbakuk 3:17 says: Although the fig tree shall not blossom, nor fruit be in the vines; the labour of the olive shall fail, and the field shall yield no meat; the flock shall be cut off from the fold, and there shall be no herd in the stalls: Yet I will rejoice in the LORD. I will joy in the God of my salvation. May God help us to see He deserves our worship always.

PRAYER: Dear Heavenly Father, You are the King of glory. You are worthy of all honour, praise and worship. Please help me to honour You with my words and actions. May my life be reflective of who You are. All power and glory belongs to You. This is my humble prayer, in Jesus Christ's mighty name.
Amen.

Lucy Ncube (3/4/22)

(15)

Dors' Camilla (bush/ tree) plant, London

(16)

6. No, not Christmas tree; but Calvary's tree!!!
(Recognition)

On the morning of 6th Jan. '22, I awoke at 5.20am for Hanworth Church Prayerline, but I'd spent all night dreaming about

Jesus on the cross on the hill!

We've just come out of Christmas 2021 celebrations. But to them I say: "Nevermind their pagan Christmas tree!

Look to Jesus on Calvary's tree
His cross borne for us His saving grace.

The true Saviour of the world
Our real Superhero!

The original 'Christ' in **Christ**mas."

All heaven sings "halleluiahs!!" at Jesus' love sacrifice for us, mankind.

I could hear angels' jubilant and melodious songs and hymns of praises like:

'For while He was on the cross, we (you and I) were on His mind'
(song by Ronald Hinson, & Ronald Michael Payne (c) 1984, Mike Payne & www.songsolutions.org BMG Chrysalis & Hal Leonard Corporation).

PRAYER & PRAISE:

Dearest Jesus, my Lord and King, my Redeemer and Saviour, **my All-in-All**, thank You for putting me on Your mind whilst You were on that cross/ tree on Calvary's hill. I'm blown away by Your immense love for me, for us, for humanity!

Let me learn, daily, to love and appreciate You more and more, amen, hallelujah!
Doreen Joseph (6/1/22)
(17)

(Niagara Falls, Canada)

(Shutterstock.com)

7. Gratitude to God
(Thanksgiving)

Psalm 75:1 (KJV) Unto thee, O God, do we give thanks, unto thee do we give thanks, for that thy name is near thy wondrous works declare.

Have you ever looked back on your life and thought about all that God has done for you? All He has provided for you, the numerous times He covered and protected you, situations He brought you through, His grace and mercy towards you? I'm sure we all have. I recall having one of those moments in 2012, I became so filled with gratitude to God, I decided to journal, mainly in an effort to capture and relish every situation that I can recall God's extraordinary acts or His wondrous works on my behalf and to give Him all the thanks. I know for certain what God can do. I know what God has done for me. Reading my journal also strengthens my faith. My recorded account of God's blessings and recalling the testimony of others, fills me with gratitude that I can put my trust in Him. If God fixed it for us in the past, He can fix it for us in the present.

I am also grateful to God for His word which fundamentally assures us of His omnipotent power and grace in every situation. His word tells us that God, who created the world in six days (Exodus 20:11), who parted the Red Sea for the children of Israel to escape Pharaoh and His army (Exodus 14), who raised Lazarus from the dead after four days (John 11) and who preserved the three Hebrew boys in the fiery furnace (Daniel 3), is the same God that is able to deliver His children with His mighty hand (Hebrews 13:8).

Prayer – Dear Heavenly Father, I am truly grateful for all that You have done for us, Your children. I am truly grateful that we can put our trust in the Creator of the universe, the ultimate way maker and problem solver. How blessed we are as Your children. Help us to always and forever have a spirit of gratitude towards You. I love You and I thank You from the depths of my heart, in Jesus' name amen.

Ruth M. Chambers (July 2022)

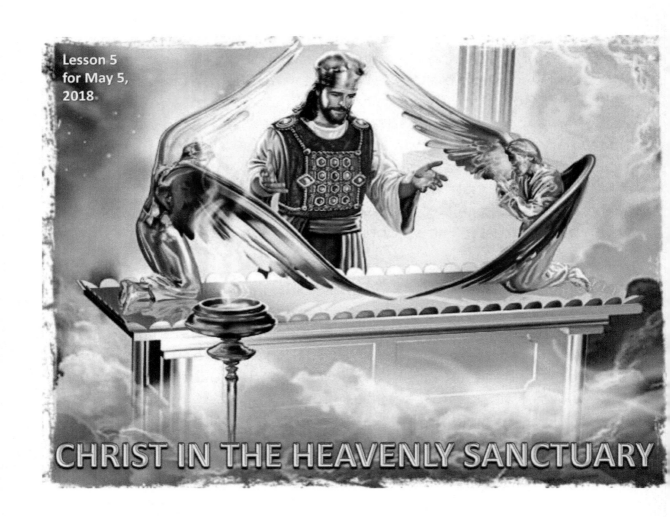

Lesson 5
for May 5,
2018

CHRIST IN THE HEAVENLY SANCTUARY

(*SDA Ellen G. White; sabbath (Saturday) school lesson)

8. Jesus Intercedes for Us
(Thanksgiving)

Romans 8:34 (KJV) ......It is Christ that died, yea rather, that is risen again, who is even at the right hand of God, who also maketh intercession for us.

Intercession is a form of prayer, albeit it goes deeper, it involves 'standing in the gap' advocating on behalf of fallen souls. Jesus the spotless lamb of God, stands in our place before God and pleads on our behalf. He alone can intercede for us. His death on the cross was the only sacrifice of value to our salvation and access to God (White, E.G. (1899).

Thank You Jesus, because of You we can commune with God through prayer. Because of You Jesus, we have the opportunity to lift up our hearts in praise to God, to thank God for His love, kindness, mercy, grace, patience, forgiveness and faithfulness. Prayer is the channel through which we can also seek God's guidance, counsel and direction and tell Him how much we love Him. This is all because of Jesus who stands in our place and intercedes on our behalf. Profoundly, the Bible tells us that we know not what we should pray as we ought, however Jesus intercedes for us according to the will of God, with groanings that cannot be uttered (Romans 8:26 & 27).

Oh, what joy and gratitude we should all have for Jesus who loves us, way beyond the comprehension of human minds. So much so, that He became the propitiation for our sins and is now in heaven at the right hand of God continuously interceding on our behalf (Hebrews 7:25).

My Prayer - Thank You God the Father and Jesus the son for loving us and for the plan of salvation. Thank You Jesus for paying the ultimate price for our sins, and for continually interceding on our behalf so that our prayers can go before the Father. Jesus, we love You and we are truly grateful to You. In Jesus' name I pray amen.

Ruth M. Chambers (March 2023)

(Steemit. 10 lepers)

9. Thanksgiving and Praise
(Thanksgiving)

Luke 17:17 NKJV: So Jesus answered and said, "Were there not ten cleansed? But where are the nine?

How do you feel when you see someone struggling? Then you go out of your way to help them, i.e. holding a door open, or protecting them from an obstacle.

How do you feel when after doing something kind, they just walk straight through without even an acknowledgement.

You might say we shouldn't do things for acknowledgment. But it is nice to receive a thank you or a nod or some sort of acknowledgment, isn't it?

You might be the one who says. That's why I don't help others, I just look out for myself.   So I have no expectations.

I believe human beings were made to be around each other to help each other. The Bible reminds us . . . Let us not become weary in doing good, for at the proper time we will reap a harvest if we do not give up. Galatians 6:9

I recall a story of Jesus healing 10 lepers of a deadly disease and only one returning to say thank you. How did He feel? He asked the question, "Where are the other 9?" Today let's give our praise and thanksgiving. Today let's find something to say thank you for.

Let us pray: Dear Heavenly Father,

At times I feel overwhelmed with life and I can not see the good things around me. Help me to pause right now and
reflect on 2 things to thank You for.

 (Take time to think and write down in a journal 2 things to say thank you for.)

(to be continued...)

(Student health services image)

I want to thank You, Papa Yahweh for the many blessings You provide me with. (Name the things on your list individually).

I thank You for _____, (pause)

I thank You so much for _____, (pause)

Papa Yahweh, You are so merciful and gracious to me.

Help me to see the precious things in life and to focus on You and doing good to help myself and to help others around me, as You also help me.

I love You.

Remove anything that would hinder You from hearing my prayer today.

Forgive me.

And help me to forgive others.

I pray in Jesus' name.

Amen 🙏

Sharon Davis (March 2023)

(Grenada, W.I.)

10. Halleluiah! Thank you, Yahweh!
(Thanksgiving)

"Give Praise and Thanksgiving to Father Yahweh, by Whom we are given uncounted mercies and countless blessings daily."
(The Holy Spirit inspired me in 2016 for the once in a lifetime occurrence that 4 generations of my family were together in Grenada).
Yes, indeed, 'give thanks and praise, for His mercy endures forever' (Psalm 136 v 1).

In Spring/Summer 2022, Yahweh enabled my daughter, my sister and I to visit Grenada to see my elderly dad, (a great grand dad) who had been ill. Jesus enabled us to put in place a care and treatment package for him too., which brought relief and peace of mind. Father Yahweh also opened other doors for us to further realise hopes and dreams being manifested.

Grenada is a beautiful 'Spice isle' that tests stamina with its 'hills and gullies' in sweltering heat, and remarkable floral perfumed delights. We reconnected with family and friends, discovered new family members, friendships, and splashed in the sandy beach combed sea. These were truly blessings from the Lord, and gratefully appreciated!

The beautiful lush flora and fauna are reminiscent of Eden's Garden, and foretaste the new earth and new heaven to be created after the present ones are consumed in fire and brimstone, after Judgement Day is passed and punishments for the unrepentant wicked ones are meted out. (EGWhite, (1947/1980) 'The Story of Redemption' chp 66, The second death, p428 - 429 citing Ps 11 v 6, Malachi 4 v1, 2 Pet. 3 v10, Is. 30 v 33, Is. 34 v 8; Rev. 20 v 13; & D. Joseph 'Perfect Circles, vol. 1' chp 9, p232 & p314 - 315, 2013).

We embrace that day of YHWH'S and Christ's righteous judgements and sanctifying, purifying fires that will eradicate sin and evil forever, and herald a new dawn, a future of perfection, holiness, joy, peace and perpetual worship in the presence of our heavenly Makers.
We 'will see YHWH face to face and not die'
(Exod. 33 v 20; yet Exod. 33 v 11 &   Rev. 22 v 4).

(to be continued.....)   (27)

(Jewish 7 candle stick)

(Shutterstock.com)

At last, because Jesus died to redeem us and has reconciled us to YHWH, we will once again have 'perfect circles relationships with YHWH' that Adam and Eve had enjoyed; this time for all Eternity! Won't that be marvellous?

On 10th July, our sister - writer, Ruth, suggested we change our book's name from 40 or 49 to '50 days devotional'. This would represent the Jewish sabbatical year when slaves were freed, and was a Jubilee celebration. It also coincided with that year, 2022, being a Platinum Jubilee year for our Queen Elizabeth II.

Then on sabbath 23rd July, I dreamt the number '7', and it was repeated 3 times ie triple 7 (777). This is the number of perfection/ completion and it is a holy number and represents YHWH's 7 Holy Spirits (Rev. 4 v 5). Its repetition was emphatic, indicating the seriousness of the holy estate, yey, even the pure, selfless, holy and ephemeral state of YHWH Himself and His Son, Jesus Christ (D. Joseph ibid. Chp 1, p6, 2013).

Praise Song:
As song 311 in SDA hymnal says 'I would be like Jesus....

Chorus:
Be like Jesus, this my song, in the home and in the throng,
Be like Jesus all day long, I would be like Jesus.'

(© 19h century James Rowe & B.D. Akler).

So let it be/ selah, my Lord and Saviour, amen.

Doreen Joseph (3rd, 10th & 23rd July '22).

(* SDA is Seventh Day Adventist Christian church)

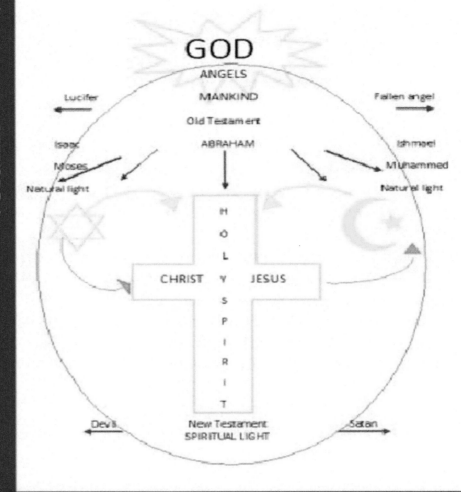

Perfect Circles
volume 1

Doreen Joseph

PERFECT CIRCLES vol 1
an exploration of faith and relationships with
YHWH (Yahweh) - our heavenly Father

Be Blessed and be a Blessing

Shrigley Hall, hotel & spa grounds, Macclesfield, Manchester

11. Blessings & Deliverance
(Blessings)

I'd like to share my testimony of how Yahweh and Jesus have blessed me, and delivered me, from nightmare situations multiple times in my life... First of all, I was born two months premature, and needed a hernia operation on my stomach during my first week of life, - dicey in 1959! I'd been plagued with various childhood illnesses, abuse, and even suicidal thoughts as a teenager, - but for hearing the Holy Spirit's voice reassuring me I would survive my torment, I'd not be here today.

Don't get me wrong, it wasn't all doom and gloom - interspersed were happy times with siblings and friends. But trauma followed me into adulthood, failed relationships and marriage, and financial insecurities that all led to nervous breakdowns - labeled schizophrenic. Varying spells in hospital, ECT, prison, and involvement of social services - it was only that I vowed to pray harder, why I was reunited with my children, and the youngest was not put up for adoption! Happily that was not our portion/ destiny.

As I hit my 30s the Holy Spirit inspired me to begin writing what turned into a trilogy - 'Perfect Circles - an exploration of faith & relationships with YHWH (Yahweh), our heavenly Father. I came under great Satanic attacks in the duration. The first book was hindered by 21 years until on 19/10/2010 Jesus showed me in a dream that He had delivered me from the tyranny of psychiatry, to fulfill my destiny, to write the trilogy in His liberty, won for me on the cross of Calvary.

Alongside mental distress came persecution from family and friends, even church family, work, home insecurity, stroke and temporary paralysis, COVID (but not hospitalised, thank the Lord) and much more,- almost too great to bear. However, Jesus carried me when I was helpless and bewildered, to have freedom to live, love and breathe and write faithfully and soul-satisfyingly; I hope to Yahweh's pleasure and glory.

(to be continued...)   (33)

Dor's flowers, London

As our family explores our history, who knows what bonds may be knit, loose ends tied up, knowledge gaps filled? But our life journey will be great and full of promise because Jesus is at the helm, and Yahweh holds us in His righteous right hand (Isaiah 41 v 10).

We will not falter, as YHWH has promised me that my children and grandchildren will come to worship Him, and call Him their Father, and He will call them His children (Isaiah 44 v 1 - 4).
Hallelujah! We praise, worship, adore and thank Them immensely.

PRAISES: All laud, glory, honour and thanksgiving are due to Jesus, the Lamb that was slain for us; and to Creator and Blessor, Yahweh. Amen.

Doreen Joseph (26/1/22).

Shrigley Hall, hotel & spa, Macclesfied, Manchester

(36)

12. Blessings - Peace, Love & Joy!
(Blessings)

We were blessed to have a Christmas break, relaxing at Shrigley Hall, Hotel & Spa, Macclesfield near Manchester, UK, 2021. We enjoyed a peaceful and delightful time, including their luxurious relaxing spa.

However, the best blessing we can have is the love, joy and peace of knowing that Yahweh loves us. And that we can bask in His glorious love, - a love that is so great that He allowed His beloved Son, Jesus, to voluntarily give up - His life for us on Calvary's cross, 2,000 years ago, (John 3 v 16 - 17).

But happily, it didn't end there. Miraculously, Jesus took up His life again, was resurrected, to return to heaven, where He prays, interceding for us sinners, to His Father, Yahweh.

Jesus had victory over the grave, over death - the curse incurred by Satan. Christ gives us hope of eternal life, where we can be in His company and presence of Jehovah, our Creator and Benefactor! We will be able to see YHWH face to face and not die! (Revelation 22 v 4) Isn't that marvellous?

Truly it'll be a blessing we can pray for, enjoy, and look forward to. Hallelujah! Halleluiahs! Jesus 'soon come' and shall not tarry (Hebrews 10 v 37 - 39). Let us be ready to greet Him, so He can take us with Him to heaven, where we will reign alongside Him as priests, judges and joint heirs to His kingdom, (1 Corinthians 6 v 2 - 3; Romans 8 v 16 - 18).

PRAISES: Dearest Jesus, thank You for giving us the hope of eternal rest, peace, relaxation, joy and love, with You and Father Yahweh, and heavenly and universal hosts and saints. You are worthy to be praised and adored, hallelujah, amen.

Doreen Joseph (24/1/22).

(Shutterstock)

'He is not here, He is risen,' (Matt. 28 v 6) Halleluiahs galore!!

Jesus the Christ's victory over death (1 Corin. 15 v 54 - 55)

13. Blessings! Amen & Amen!
(Blessings)

"I will not let you go, unless you bless me!" said Jacob to the angel he wrestled with at Peniel, on his way to reconcile with his brother Esau. He was then renamed "Israel" because he wrestled with (YHWH) and prevailed. (Genesis 32 v 24 - 28).

In these very present times, we need to ask the Lord to bless us with an abundance .. (not merely like Jabez prayed, to be blessed and enlarge his territory, 1 Chronicles 4 v 10); but to increase our faith, patience, endurance and love! Persecution is approaching, is even already upon us, with the enforcement of COVID vaccines; and very soon imposition of Sunday law - to be permitted to worship only on Sundays; in opposition to YHWH's true sabbath - sunset Friday to sunset Saturday!

It is a very taxing, stressful and frightening time for Yahweh's 4th commandment/ sabbath keepers - 7th Day Adventists. Yet we need not be afraid, but courageous! "Do not fear, I AM with you. I will uphold you with My righteous right hand," says the Lord (Isaiah 41 v 10). How huge must His caring hand be! How immense is His love to hold us in the palm of His hand, - all the saints and the saved elect!!!

Jesus promised to be ever with us, even to the end of the earth (Matt. 28 v 20). Nor will He or Yahweh abandon or forsake us. They sent us the Holy Spirit, afterall, to guide and comfort us, (John 14 v 16).

They say: "be strong and courageous, don't be afraid," (Deutoronomy 31 v 6; Hebrews. 13 v 5). 'Hold fast to what you know, your faith in Christ (Revelation 3 v 11), to His truth, that you may be saved and delivered, and receive your crown, laurel and harp (Rev. 2 v 10 & 14 v 1 - 5; James 1 v 12; E. G. White, 'The Great Controversy' chp 40, p645, 646; & EGW. 'Last Day Events' chp 19, p282); and sit at the marriage feast of Lamb / victorious Jesus Christ; (Rev. 19 v 7 - 10).

PETITION: please fashion and equip us with courage, strength, patience and endurance, ever in the hope of Your deliverance and rewards, dear Father Yahweh, inspired and led by our forerunner Jesus, the Christ, amen.

Doreen Joseph (24/1/22).   (39)

(Shutterstock)

14. Blessings Galore!
(Blessings)

'Bless the Lord, O my soul, and forget not all His benefits!' (Psalm 103 v 1)

Blessings come from above; indeed they come from Yahweh's love!

What does He say?
Yahweh says He longs to give us the gift of the Holy Spirit, more than parents who are evil/ sinners give good gifts to their children. (Matt. 7 v 11; Luke 11 v 13). That says a lot!

In fact He has already given us the greatest gift ever - His Son, Jesus Christ, to redeem us / buy us back from evil Satan, by His death on Calvary's cross. He is our Saviour from trials and tribulations to come, especially when He returns as a rewarder and avenger, at the End of Time (very soon from now). Whose side will you be on, His or the devil's? I pray we are on the winning side - Christ's.

Yes, indeed, Yahweh promises to bless us exceeding abundantly, (Ephesians 3 v 10 - 21), if we obey His commandments/ laws, and have the testimony of 'the Lamb', His Son, Jesus Christ, (Revelation 12 v 11 & v 17). Let us pray for endurance and patience of the saints, (Revelation 14 v 12), so we can stand, and still stand (Ephesians 6 v 13) during persecution.

In 2011, the Holy Spirit gave me 4 messages, as my daughters were preparing to be baptised SDA, - truly a jubilant day in my life!   One message was:

"Rejoice! For our Lord, Jesus Christ has died and is risen to save us, halleluiah!"

In 2016, the Holy Spirit gave me another message, when Yahweh had enabled 4 generations of our family to spend Christmas together in Grenada:

"Give praise and thanksgiving for Father Yahweh, by Whom we are given uncounted mercies and countless blessings daily."

PRAISES: Yes, I will bless the Lord, O my soul, For Yahweh's plentiful blessings!
Doreen Joseph (3 & 13/1/22).   (41)

Hanging basket, Kew Gardens, London

You can hang on to / trust the Lord

(42)

Faithfulness and Trust

Photoshot by Mercedes

(44)

15. God is Faithful to Those who Seek Him
(God's faithfulness)

Psalm 34:10 (KJV) ......but those who seek the Lord lack no good thing.

God has proven, time and time again, that He is faithful to those who seek Him. Friends, whatever you're going through, take it to the Lord in prayer, He will NEVER fail You. God wants us to acknowledge Him in all things, no matter how trivial the situation may appear (1 Peter 5 v 7). Lean not on your own understanding or the understanding of others; seek God's guidance, counsel and direction; acknowledge God (Proverbs 3:5-6)! This will enable His anointing and blessings to follow you, in everything you do.

Life may not always be perfect, or situations turn out the way we want them to. Notwithstanding, it will work out for the good of those who seek the Lord. Remember, God's love for us is unparalleled. His love for us far exceeds that of mother, father, children, friend and the love we have for ourselves. Thus, we cannot out want or out do God's goodness towards us. Equally God's wisdom is unmatched, His wisdom is far beyond our comprehension (Isaiah 55:9, 1 Corinthians 1:25). So, trust when we seek God in prayer and He answers yes, no, wait or in a way that we don't understand, it is always for our good; be it to keep us from straying away from Him, to draw us closer to Him, to strengthen our faith or He has something better in store for us.
God is forever faithful to those who seek Him.

My Prayer - Dear Father in Heaven, thank You for Your faithfulness to all who seek You. Help us to always trust Your love for us and Your wisdom. When we come to You in prayer, please remind us Father that You will not withhold any good from those who seek and acknowledge You in all things. In Jesus' name I pray amen.

Ruth M. Chambers (March 2022)

(Shutterstock)

16. Great is Thy Faithfulness.
(God's faithfulness)

What a mighty God we serve! Apart from creating us in His image He loves us with an everlasting love. He is so faithful in everything. He promised to redeem us from the darkness into His marvellous light. He fulfilled this promise when He gave us His only begotten Son to die on the cross for our transgressions. Christ redeemed us through His blood.

When Thomas Obadia Chisholm wrote the uplifting hymn 'Great is Thy Faithfulness' based on Lamentations 3:22-23 which reads :22-Because of the LORD's great love, we are not consumed, for His compassions never fail. 23: They are new every morning; great is Your faithfulness (NIV),he had seen how God had been there through all seasons.

The writer continues to write "There is no shadow of turning with Thee" We can be assured that God is the same yesterday, today and forever.

This song has given me hope over the years when things seemed to be crumbling down, when I lost close family members to death, lost a job, or when it looked like nothing could change. There were times I thought I couldn't go on, I had no strength left in me. If it had not been for God I would have perished. I sought the LORD and He comforted me. He gave me peace not as man gives but as only He can give. With that He provided me with my church family, work colleagues, and new opportunities, as I held on to Philippians 4:13 which reads. "I can do all things through Christ who strengtheneth me"(KJV).

Man will promise one thing and do exactly the opposite at times and we remain baffled. We need to go to our Father Yahweh first, not man, because He is faithful and just. When we go to man first we are not trusting that God will come through for us. When faced with trying times we need to 'let go and let God' take control of any situation.

Some situations may seem enormous, high mountains, and it's in those times that we should seek to see with our faith. When the sickness will not heal,, your eyesight is failing, when you lose your job, no job offers, when the
(to be continued...)

(47)

The Ark of the Covenant

(Shutterstock)

children turn away from God, when bills pile up, when debt is insurmountable and creditors are knocking on your door, when you are stuck in your studies, in your business, just cry out to the LORD;

just like King Hezekiah, who received and read letters brought by Rabshakeh from his master the king of Assyria, that he went up to the house of the LORD, and spread it before the LORD. "Then Hezekiah prayed before the LORD and said "O LORD God of Israel, the One who dwells between the cherubim, You alone are God over all the kingdoms of the earth. You have made heaven and earth. Incline Your ear, O LORD and hear, open Your eyes, O LORD and see and hear the words of Sennacherib, which he has sent to reproach the living God. Truly LORD, the kings of Assyria have laid waste the nations and their lands, and have cast their gods, but the work of men's hands-wood and stone. Therefore they destroyed them. Now therefore, O LORD our God, I pray, save us from his hand, that all the kingdoms of the earth may know that You are the LORD God, You alone'" 2 Kings 19: 14-19.(KJV).

Now let's hear how God answered: "Because you have prayed to Me, against Sennacherib, king of Assyria, I have heard'". Hallelujah,
read the whole passage and see the outcome for yourself.

My dear friends - Great is His Faithfulness, our God our Father. He will anoint your head with oil in the presence of your enemies, (Psalm 23 v 5).

PRAYER:

Our kind and loving Father in heaven, we glorify Your name above all names. We exalt Your name on high. You alone are God and besides You there is no other. You are forever faithful. You are the Alpha and the Omega.

Forgive us for the times we have not come to You first, and sometimes gone to our friends and family for answers and then only come to You when all else has failed.

Help us through Your Holy Spirit to trust You and Your precepts. Only You can give us a heart of flesh instead of a heart of stone.
Thank You for all the blessings You have given and continue to give us.
I love You LORD, in Jesus Christ mighty name. Amen

Lucy Ncube (2/8/22)   (49)

(Shutterstock)

17. Uncertain Days
(Faith/Trust)

"Trust in the Lord with all thine heart; and lean not unto thine own understanding. In all thy ways acknowledgeHim, and He shall direct thy paths". (Proverbs 3:5,6)

In these days of uncertainty - when all seems difficult and hard to figure out; when the outgoings are more than the incomings, it makes you think what does the future really hold?   It seems like worries continually occupy the mind. Just a kind reminder God is already in your tomorrows. He already knows the way. Why? Because He has a plan for your life.   All He wants you to do is trust in Him with all your heart. You can be assured the plan He has for you is the best plan ever.

You must remember that God has not, and will not, ask you to figure it out all alone. He just wants you to recognise that He is sovereign Lord, and that you can trust Him, and without a shadow of a doubt He shall direct your path. Trust, trust, trust, Him completely, today.

PRAYER:

Father, You are God of my life, help me to trust You for directions, trust You because You are Sovereign Lord, You can take care of everything in my life when I allow You to direct my path.

Debbie Jones (Jan. '22)

Beehive plant in Kew Gardens, London by Dors

18. Resilience in Adversity
(Trust)

For I know the plans I have for you," declares the Lord, "plans to prosper you and not to harm you, plans to give you hope and a future. Bible Version: NIV Jeremiah 29:11

Ever made plans that didn't work out?
Worked hard for something you then did not receive? Believed in someone's promise, which isn't kept. I'll be one of the first to say it isn't easy. With all the good will, love, trust in the world. Sometimes things just don't work out just quite as we expected.

However, I would also be in the group that says: "All things work together for good." I've come to realise that just like a parent does not want bad things to happen to the child they love. But that child will run and fall down, scraping their knee, breaking a bone, crying. That loving parent is there to wipe away the tears, encouraging progress, supporting that child to get back up and to keep going.

Our Heavenly Father is that person to us. He cares enough to be there when we fall down. Be there when we ugly cry and in our worst stages of whatever we are in. He will remain right there. His dreams for us do not diminish. But the experience shapes us to be more of who He created us to be, if we trust the process.

Sometimes we just cannot see the big picture and things may look bleak.

But.......

He has a plan for us. "For I know the plans I have for you (___ Put your name here ___) declares the Lord, plans to prosper you and not to harm you, plans to give you hope and a future.

Let's Pray:
Dear Heavenly Father,

Today as I contemplate the hard knocks of life. help me to feel your love
(to be continued....)
(53)

Carol's Chinese Tiger lilies, London

Help me to realise that the important lessons of building resilience, being stronger
in the times of adversity and hard times. Help me to become the best version of me. So that I can fulfill my purpose for you. Help me to trust you.
Lord help my unbelief. (Pause)

Protect me, guide me and remove all that you don't want me to experience right now. But keep me focused on you and not on anything that is happening around me.

Forgive me and Save me today. (Pause)
In Jesus' name I pray.
Amen 🙏

Sharon Davis (March 2023)

(Hannah's bee)

19. Casting and Searching
(Faith/Trust)

'Casting all your cares upon Him for He careth for you', (1 Peter 5:7). 'And ye shall seek Me and find Me when ye shall search for Me with all your heart', (Jeremiah 29:13).

Today the word speaks " casting your cares upon Him for He cares for you". Choosing to place your faith and trust in God will be to you peace and assurance. Choosing to take Him at His word will give you assurance and blessings.

Jeremiah advises you to seek and find Him by searching for Him with all your heart. This search means studying His divine words and asking Him to help you get to know Him. In other words, surrender your will and be devoted to a knowledge of Him.

You see, in this world you'll never find a return or investment of faith and trust in anything else as you would in God. He is able to take your faith and trust and multiply them, so that you'll find great rewards in the things you trust Him with.

You see you'll find true satisfaction, peace and joy in God when you have learned to trust Him with all your heart.

PRAYER:

O Father, today I place my confidence in Your word as I cast all my cares upon You. I am choosing to search for You through Your divine words. May you bless me abundantly in Jesus Name. Amen

Debbie Jones (Jan. '22).

(Shutterstock)

(58)

20. My God changes not
(Faithfulness)

He changes not.

Lamentations 3:22-23 "The steadfast love of the LORD never ceases; His mercies never come to an end; they are new every morning; great is Your faithfulness."(ESV)

Every morning as I watch the grass, the trees and all the plants whatever season, summer, autumn, winter and spring, I marvel at what nature teaches us that for everything there's a season. All the plants 🌱 and trees know how to wait for spring

So many times I have gone through different seasons and at times I have not been as patient as nature. I have even tried to do things my way. I have even had my Jonah moments where I have not always prayerfully listened to that small voice.

I am so glad that God never changes, He never ceases to amaze me. Sometimes when I am just about to give up, He shows up in miraculous ways.

One of those times is when I thought I had lost an important document and I had looked everywhere. I had not seen the document for over a year as I didn't need it at the time. I was just about to give up even though this meant I was going to miss an important opportunity. I was very certain that I was never going to find it.

Later that day I had a hunch to put my coat in my car boot. As I opened the car boot I couldn't believe that the document I had been looking for was so visibly staring at me. This was not the first time, but one of many and I believe there is still more to come.

God is faithful and He answers even before we ask. Let's look to nature and learn to prayerfully wait on the LORD, who will renew our strength.

PRAYER::
Dear Heavenly Father, thank You for your faithfulness, thank You for Your mercies endure forever, thank You for Your endless love.

(to be continued..)

(59)

Breadfruit tree in Grenada, W.I.

(60)

Father thank You for reminding us to wait on You in all seasons just as the trees, the grass and the plants. Help us to trust in You.

Forgive us LORD when we have tried to do things on our own. We acknowledge that heaven and earth are the LORD's and all that is within.

Thank You for listening to my prayer. In Jesus Christ mighty name, Amen

Lucy Ncube (June '22)

(Shutterstock)

21. Great is thy faith
(Grace)

"And behold, a woman of Canaan came out of the same coasts, and cried unto Him, saying, " have mercy on me, O Lord, Thou son of David; my daughter is grievously vexed with a devil". Then Jesus answered and said unto her, "O woman, great is thy faith: be it unto thee even as thou wilt." And her daughter was made whole from that very hour".
(Matthew 15:21-28.)

Wherever Jesus went He brought with Him love and grace. However there were those who constantly challenged Him. That is, Jesus always challenged boundaries and pushed for religious leaders to understand that we are all sinners in need of grace.

A Canaanite woman was His encounter. Jesus made it known that she was not an Israelite, and that it was not His business to heal her daughter. So Jesus said, "It is not right to take the children's bread and toss it to the dogs". This non- Israelite woman was clever, bold and brave, and challenged Jesus by saying "even the dogs eat the crumbs that fall from their master's table".

Jesus had his mission and that was to fulfill God's promise to all who would believe. Jesus' mission was not just to save the Israelites, and the woman's answer stated by faith that Jesus' mission was to save not only Israel, but the whole world.

Jesus knew that the woman had great faith, and He was happy that this woman expressed it. Jesus granted the woman her request: her daughter was made well that very moment. Jesus offers grace that is extensive. It is for us to accept it, and give thanks. Amazing grace.

PRAYER:

Dear Father of life, thanks for Your amazing grace that is extended to all.
Bless You, Father, amen.

Debbie Jones (Jan. 22).

Lake Grand Etang, Grenada, W.I.

22. NO PRAYER WASTED
(Patience)

The children of Israel waited for over 400 years to be delivered from the Egyptians. They had been praying for generations and generations and some must have given up hope when God sent Moses to deliver them. They questioned Moses not believing he had been sent by God.

Sometimes it might look like God is not answering our prayers. We might have prayed for that particular request for years and years. We look around us and we see others receiving their answers and blessings and we get discouraged thinking God has skipped our prayer request, or that He has pushed them back or not even listened to them.
We could be praying for healing, relationship restoration, spiritual growth, financial blessings.

The problem with us is that we try to fit God into our human understanding. We forget that God's thoughts are not our thoughts, neither are our ways His ways, declares the LORD. For as the heavens are higher than the earth so are His ways higher than our ways, and His thoughts than our thoughts, (Isaiah 55 v 8 - 9). In 2 Peter 3:8 we read: " But do not forget this one thing, dear friends with the LORD a day is like a thousand years and a thousand years like a day."

When we see other people's prayers answered immediately and we are disheartened, the Psalmist encourages us in Psalm 40:1 when he said "I waited on the LORD. He inclined to me and heard my cry". Again the wisest king Solomon also writes in Ecclesiastes 7:8 "The end of something is better than its beginning. Patience is better than pride."

We should never give up on our Father Yahweh.

I believe we all know of people whose prayers were answered when they had even forgotten that they even prayed for those blessings.
God is faithful. He is good, and wants everything that is good for you and me.

God answers prayers sometimes immediately and at other times before we even utter one word in prayer, He answers. Then again at times He will not give us what we asked for, because He knows what is best for us. He might tell us to wait because when we wait on the LORD because
(to be continued..)

Annandale waterfall, Grenada, W.I.

(66)

He promises to "renew our strength, we will run and not get weary, we will walk and not faint." (Isaiah 40 v 31).

God will even work out things we haven't prayed for yet.

He is God over everything. Therefore let us not grow weary of waiting, and as we continue to wait and be obedient to His Word, we will soon find out that "No prayer is ever wasted".

Let's talk to God before doing anything else.

And let's remember God when we get what we prayed for.

Prayer:

Dear Heavenly Father, I thank You that You are God over everything. Besides You there is no other. I glorify Your mighty name.

I pray that You would forgive us of our impatience and immaturity.

I thank You that You have never given up on us. I thank You that You answer all prayers.

I pray that You would give us strength to endure and encouragement to wait on You. I pray that You would help us to remember You when all that we ask for has come to pass.

I pray all this in the only powerful name of Jesus Christ.

Lucy Ncube (July 2022)

Kalifi, Kenya by Alithea.

23. Faith in the Midst of Growth.
(Faith)

Mark 11:22 (KJV) And Jesus answering saith unto them, Have faith in God.

I prayed for the job I now have. I prayed not my will but Your will dear Father. I believe God answered my prayers and paved the way.
So why do I become discouraged when faced with challenges?

The Holy Spirit revealed to me that my Heavenly Father is developing me into spiritual wholeness. Thus, He will put me in situations that require my trust in Him; my trust in His process. I am learning daily to
have faith in the midst of my growth.

There will be situations in life that are challenging, although you are where God ordained you to be. I am reminded that Moses faced many challenges, notwithstanding, he was called to lead the children of Israel out of Egypt (Exodus 17:4). The road won't always be easy. However, my experience has been, and I wholeheartedly believe, that the will of God will not take you, where the grace of God cannot keep you. It is God's grace that will give you wisdom and understanding. It is God's grace that will give you favour. It is God's grace that will give you strength and endurance. It is God's grace that will give you whatever help you need, to overcome challenges and to achieve success.

My Prayer - Thank You Heavenly Father, for every dream and ambition that You have placed in my heart. Thank You for answered prayers. Thank You for Your many blessings. Thank You for loving me and for tenderly working on me and developing me into spiritual wholeness. I love You and I am truly grateful. Help me to always put my trust in You. I pray that my faith in You will never fail so that I can be used by You to testify of Your goodness. Help me to continue to grow in You, in Jesus' name I pray amen.

Ruth M. Chambers (February 2022)

Limecross nursery, East Sussex

24. He has never failed me yet.
(YHWH's faithfulness)

Moving into a new neighbourhood can cause anxiety.
One of our priorities when looking for a house was a quiet neighbourhood, friendly neighbours, private parking space, as well as gardening space. We had rented a house near a new shopping centre and this could be noisy at times, hence we were looking for a quiet area.

We had found some houses with the perfect specs, though they all fell through. However, the one we finally settled for seemed the exact opposite of what we were looking for. We live next door to a primary school, parking is communal, and one could get blocked. Apart from one friendly neighbour the others were not so welcoming initially.

All things work together for good (Romans 8 v 28). A few months later, we appreciated the blessing of living next to a school. During school holidays we noticed we were missing the chatter and the happy voices. The neighbours had got used to us and they are all friendly and supportive.
No one blocks our car.

As time went on the neighbours noticed that we go to church on a Saturday. Most of them didn't understand why we go on Saturday instead of Sunday.

We have always prayed for our neighbourhood as in 1 Timothy 2:1 which reads "I exhort therefore, that, first of all, supplications, prayers, intercessions and giving of thanks , be made for all men". Other people asked if we could invite them over to our church. We also offered prayers for those who requested.

I now know why the LORD allowed us to live in this neighbourhood. We are so grateful that God knows from the end to the beginning (Isaiah 46 v 9 - 11).

As I look into His word I cannot help but think of God providing a lamb to Abraham instead of Isaac (Genesis 22 v 1 - 19). I think of how He provided for the children of Israel throughout the wilderness giving them manna for food, (Exodus 16 v 4 - 36). It's amazing how God will never leave us nor forsake us. God has never failed me yet.

(to be continued...)

Bougainvillea flowers, Grenada, W.I.

PRAYER:

Our dear Heavenly Father,
I glorify Your name.
The Psalmist sums it up that "Your name is a strong tower and the righteous run to You and are saved" (Proverbs 18 v 10).

Thank You for not leaving me nor forsaking me.

Forgive me for the times I have not fully trusted in your provision. Like the children of Israel, I am guilty of not putting my whole trust in You when I am having issues of life.

Thank You for Your Holy Spirit who guides me. I pray all this in no other name but the most powerful name of Jesus Christ. Amen

Lucy Ncube, (10/8/22)

Prayer 2

Father Yahweh,
Please keep me safe,
Protect and look after me.
Send your angels to shield me.
Send your Holy Spirit to guide me.
Lord, I love You,
Thank You.

25. Put on the Whole Armour of God
(God's armour)

Ephesians 6:11 (KJV) Put on the whole armour of God, that ye may be able to stand against the wiles of the devil.

As followers of Christ, we are assailed by temptations on every side. The Bible tells us that we wrestle not against flesh and blood (Ephesians 6:12). Thus, we cannot of ourselves stand against the wiles of the enemy. We are only conquerors through our Heavenly Father and by putting on the whole armour of God.

So how do we put on the whole armour of God?
We put on the belt of truth by believing and declaring the word of God to be the truth. We put on the breastplate of righteousness by obeying the word of God which is our righteousness. We put on the shoes of the gospel of peace when we remain in readiness to share the good news of the gospel of peace. We put on the shield of faith by having confidence in what we hope for and assurance in what we do not see. We put on the helmet of salvation when we protect our minds (the first point of attack) from doubt and walk in confidence of our salvation. We put on the sword of the spirit/word of God when we depend on God's word and carry His word, power and authority into every situation or conflict (Ephesians 6:14-17).

Fundamentally, we must remain persistent in prayer and supplication to be equipped with the whole armour of God (Ephesians 6:18). We will then find that the angels of God will guide, protect and surround us to withstand the wiles of the enemy, and having done all, to stand (Ephesians 6:13).

My Prayer - Thank You Heavenly Father, for every provision that You have made available for us to overcome the enemy. Help us to never trust in our own strength, but to prayerfully put on the whole armour of God so that we can stand as conquerors against the enemy. Thank You for loving us, we love You in return. In Jesus' name I pray amen.

Ruth M. Chambers (March 2023)

(Shutterstock)

26. Let God Fight Your Battles
(Trust)

2 Chronicles 20:17 (KJV) Ye shall not need to fight in this battle, set yourselves, stand ye still, and see the salvation of the Lord......

There have been periods in my life where the going got really tough, one problem arose after another. I felt so many forces coming against me, I felt spent and overwhelmed. I knew by myself I was weak and helpless.

However, I trusted God and I knew that my deliverance and salvation would come from Him and God has never failed me. He prepared a table before me in the presence of mine enemies, my cup ran over. God has a way of showing us who is God.

God doesn't want us to depend on our own strength, He desires us to put our trust in Him (2 Corinthians 12:9). Tell God about it, take Him at His word and He will move powerfully on your behalf, He will fix it (Proverbs 30:5).

Stand still and see the salvation of the Lord, He will fight your battles. I know of a certainty that God is bigger than any problem, person or authority you have or will ever come against. No force in heaven or on earth can stand against my God. For I know that my redeemer liveth, and that He shall stand at the latter day upon the earth (Job 19:25).

Prayer - Dear Father in Heaven, it's a privilege to know that we can put our trust in You. I thank You that in our weakness, You are strong. I thank You for fighting our battles and for moving powerfully on our behalf. I thank You for never failing us and for all that You have done for us. I am overwhelmed by Your love and goodness towards us. Help us to never stop putting our trust in You. Lord, we love You and we praise You for who You are,
in Jesus' name I pray, amen.

Ruth M. Chambers (July 2022)

Carol's marigolds, London

(78)

Grace and Encouragement

Chinese lilies, London

(80)

27. Our God of Mercies and grace
(Grace)

**'Blessed be God, even the Father of our Lord Jesus Christ, the Father of mercies, and the God of all comfort; who comforteth us in all our tribulation, that we may be able to comfort them which are in any trouble, by the comfort wherewith we ourselves are comforted of God'.
(2 Corinthians 1:3-4)**

We all start the New Year from the first of January. However, having begun the New Year doesn't mean that our life circumstances have changed in any way, shape or form. Maybe you have entered the New Year with all the cares you had in the old. It may be a rocky marriage, children who are disobedient, problems at work, financial difficulties, noisy neighbours, sickness and the list continues. But, it doesn't mean it should end the same.

It may seem that God is far away and your prayers are not being heard. Today I want you to be comforted in the glorious grace of God. The scripture text today reminds us that God is the Father of mercies and grace, and the God of all comfort, Who comforts us in all our afflictions.

Life at times may be challenging, life at times may throw us lemons, but we can turn these lemons into lemonade!
What a way to see life, when we change our sadness into joy. Amen, Halleluiah!

All we need to do is keep holding on to God and His words of truth and grace. This will give us sufficient strength to keep holding on.

PRAYER: The God of grace will comfort you. He will come to your aid when you ask His presence to be near. Never doubt. Just trust Him. Selah.

Debbie Jones (Jan. '22).

You are precious and special in My sight,

I love you.

–God

(internet)

28. God's Grace to us
(Grace)

"For sin shall not have dominion over you: for ye are not under the law, but under grace. But God be thanked, that ye were the servants of sin, but ye have obeyed from the heart that form of doctrine which was delivered to you...but now being made free from sin, and become servants to God, ye have your fruit unto holiness, and the end everlasting life".
(Romans 6 v 14 - 23).

There are times when you stumble, when you fail, and feel that God will never listen because you've done so many wrong deeds, and here's just another to add to the list. You feel that there's no hope for you, and that God must be very angry. How can you find grace from God yet again?

God wants you to know that He cares, and there's hope for you. The Apostle Paul makes it clear in Romans 6.   That God's grace is sufficient for you. His grace to you is precious, much more than gold. For, there's nothing that can compare. Just receive it. Make this gift yours. Do not let it go in vain.

The fact that your conscience speaks to you, and you're grieved over your wrongdoing is evidence that God's grace is still with you. His Holy spirit is active in your life. Trust that He cares for you.

PRAYER:

Dear Heavenly Father, how great you are!   I thank You that Your grace is always extended towards mankind.

May we trust in You Who so freely forgives and extends Your grace.
Let it be so, Amen.

Debbie Jones (Jan. '22).

(Shutterstock)

29. Offering of Grace
(Grace)

"For as often as ye eat this bread, and drink this cup, ye do shew the Lord's death till He comes". (1 Corinthians 11:26)

At communion we celebrate. We extend the Lord's blessings, we share the story of Jesus to all, and welcome everyone to take part in this wonderful meal. Simple as it may be, its meaning is very significant.

I look at the excitement of the disciples getting ready for the Passover Feast together. They would have reflected on other feast times spent with Jesus. They may have wondered what this feast would be like with Jesus in the upper room.

They may have recalled Jesus talking to them about His death and resurrection, which they had not yet fully understood. They had many a conversation with the Saviour, witnessed many a healing and the joy it brought to the receivers.

However, here they are at the table, and Jesus offers them the new concept, something they, and we, would follow: " As often as ye do this..."
It's something to be remembered, something to always do to remember Him by. He left us an example that we can come to Him and be renewed by His grace.

The disciples later understood that Jesus wanted all mankind to be saved by His saving grace. And that the Kingdom of God will include everyone who accepts Him as their Saviour. That's why Communion is extended to all, and no one is exempt from His saving grace. How wonderful is our Saviour!

PRAYER:

Dear Heavenly Father, help us always to remember what you did for us. And all who accept your saving grace can have eternal life. We give you thanks, amen.

Debbie Jones (Jan. 22).

(Shutterstock)

Yahweh and Jesus are our strong tower, our refuge, safe haven.

Share His Word with others so all may know Him

30. Showing Grace to Others
(Grace)

"And among the cities which ye shall give unto the Levites there shall be six cities for refuge, which ye shall appoint for the manslayer, that he may flee thither: and to them ye shall add forty and two cities" (Joshua 20).

There were six cities given as places of refuge. Three on the side of Jordan and three on the side of Canaan. God gave the order that these cities be given just in case should someone kill another accidentally, he had a place of refuge until his case was heard and a decision made.

These cities can be seen as cities of refuge. These cities can be seen as a place of rest, a place of grace given by God.

As recipients of the grace of God, *we* must be seen as places of refuge, where people who are broken, who are depressed, who are seeking hope can turn to for support in their time of need.

Many people living in our world today need a place to settle and find rest. Can your home be a place of refuge? Are our churches places that are welcoming to souls who need forgiveness and healing?

We are to be willing to reach out with God's love and grace to them, giving love and assurance in their most desperate times of need.

PRAYER:

Heavenly Father, help us to extend Your grace to others as You extend Your grace to us. May we show mercy to all who need it.

Thank You for always being there when we need You most. May we become places of refuge for others in their most desperate times.
Hear this prayer, dear Heavenly Father. Amen.

Debbie Jones (Jan. 22).

Kalifi, Kenya by Alithea

(88)

31. Suffering - No Pass for Christian
(Encouragement)

"Yea, though I walk through the valley of the shadow of death, I will fear no evil: for Thou art with me; Thy rod and they staff they comfort me". (Psalm 23:4) "Let your conversation be without covetousness; and be content with such things as ye have, for He hath said I will never leave thee, nor forsake thee.". (Hebrews 13:5)

There are times when we are facing insurmountable pressure. These pressures may come in various forms, too many bills and too little money, work related issues, medical illnesses, domestic problems, etc. I do certainly know this: that no matter how bad the situation, God's grace is able to carry you through. Remember, 'though, you walk through the valley of the shadow of death, He is with you'.

What great words of comfort, words of assurance, God will never leave you! He will be with you to the very end. Trust in Him. Even when all seems too much for you. Sometimes we expect great things to happen in big ways. Do you remember the story of Gideon, from an army of 125,000 God brought it down to 300 and the battle was won? (Judges 7).

Remember David the little shepherd boy who King Saul and his brothers thought were no match to the giant Goliath? (1 Samuel 17). God used this little shepherd boy to defeat the great giant. Trust in the Lord with all your heart. No problem is too big for him to fix. Remember being a Christian does not exempt you from trials, does not exempt you from facing difficult situations. They come to make you depend on Him. Just stay connected; trust Him. He will see you through your trials.

God always stands on His promises, He does not lie. "I will never leave thee nor forsake thee" (Deuteronomy 31 v 6; Hebrews 13 v 5) are His words of assurance; trust in His divine words.

Prayer:

O dear Father, sometimes I fail to trust You. Sometimes I forget the many stories of faith in Your words. Sometimes I even forget that You have promised, "You will never leave me".
Help me always to remember You are with me at all times,
even when facing difficult periods.
All I have to do is call on You.
Debbie Jones (Feb. 22).   (89)

(Shutterstock)

32. Held captive..
(Liberty/ Grace)

"Oh lord, set me free!", the captive; "Oh no, I will not let you go," the Deliverer.

Exodus 5- 15 tells how YHWH delivered the Israelites by Moses from stubborn Pharaoh, Rameses II, who refused to 'let His people go', until YHWH humbled him with a deathly blow to the firstborn in Egypt. But if we assume that the Deliverer is Yahweh, why does He refuse to release the captive?

Jump forward about 3 millenia to see that Yahweh's Son, Jesus Christ, 'set the captive free', all of mankind who were in bondage to sin, death and arch enemy Satan. We are set free on the liberty of Christ righteousness, when He ransomed us from Satan, by voluntarily accepting a criminal's death penalty on Calvary's cross.

Prophet Isaiah foretold this in Is. 61 v 1; and It's repeated in Luke 4 v 18. - Jesus set the captive free. He said, "he who believes in Me is free indeed,", "you will know the truth, and the truth will set you free", (John 8 v 32 - 36; and Romans 6 v 18). He and Father Yahweh give life, and do so exceedingly abundantly, (John 10 v 10; Ephes. 3 v 20 - 21). So do not be yoked again in sin, but stand firm on Christ's liberty that He won for us at Calvary, (Gals. 5 v 1).

Now that Christ paid such a huge priceless ransom, even His own precious life-giving blood, why would He release us back into the slavery of sin, to be evil Satan's captives, and death's prisoners again?

"You are Mine, " YHWH said, "fear not, I have redeemed you. I have called / summoned you by your name; you are Mine." (Isaiah 43 v 1). We belong to YHWH by Creation, and to Christ by Redemption, and Salvation. How comforting is that thought/ knowledge! Be free indeed, in Christ!

THANKSGIVING:
Dearest Father Yahweh and precious Jesus, today we heard on prayer line 20/2/22, that sister Carol's son-in-law, David, has been discharged from hospital, after being in a coma for a few weeks and in recovery for months. Thank You for delivering him from the bondage of a coma, to return to his loving, believing family. Gratefully we receive your blood-stained liberty that frees us to have 'Perfect Circle relationships with (You) YHWH'.

Doreen Joseph (20/2/22)

Edenic waterfalls, Asia

(Shutterstock)

33. He swore! Truly...
(Fidelity/ Grace)

Hebrews 6 v 17 - 18 says 'thus YHWH, determining to show more abundantly to the heirs of the promise the immutability of His counsel, confirmed it by an *oath*, ...which also is immutable/ unchangeable, being impossible for Him to lie, that we may have strong consolation and hope.' YHWH and Jesus Christ are truth, and do not, indeed, cannot lie!

YHWH swore an oath/ made a covenant/ agreement/ contract between mankind and Himself, that was a renewal and improvement on His earlier ones made with Adam, Noah, Abraham, David and others. (SDA Quarterly '22)

Because of Jesus' new covenant, ratified by His body and blood sacrificed on Calvary's cross, YHWH could make this immutable oath. His Son, Jesus' perfect life of obedience, sinlessness and perfection; even Him being the perfect atoning sacrifice to sanctify/ cleanse away/ eradicate all of our sins, once and for all, meant YHWH could then promise this particular oath. He would make Jesus a high priest after the order of Melchizedek (king and high priest of Salem), who both have no beginning or end, and are eternal, (Gen. 14 v 18 - 20; psalm 110 v 4; Hebs, 7 v 1 - 3; Rev. 1 v 8, v11; Rev. 21 v 6; Rev. 22 v 13).

YHWH's oath that He swore on Jesus' obedient, perfect blood sacrifice, guarantees His believers and followers the surety/ certainty of salvation (saved from great tribulation, and the second death in the lake of fire and brimstone, after Judgment Day). Thereby He promises eternal life, which is our hope.

Jesus is the anchor of our hope,
as our forerunner, enabling us to come behind the veil, of inner sanctuary, holiest of holies, into YHWH's holy presence, (Hebs. 4 v 16; 1 Peter 2 v 9), and not die, because Christ's perfect righteousness covers/ cleanses our guilty shameful sin.
YHWH can once again tabernacle with us - the saved, (Rev. 21 v 3-4; & Rev, 22 v 2 - 3); as He did with the Israelites in the Exodus wilderness; even as He socialised with Adam and Eve in Eden's garden.

PRAYER: Heavenly Father, Yahweh, I accept and welcome such an oath: You guaranteed the promise of salvation and eternal life, because of Jesus. Thank You, and bless Your holy name, amen.

Doreen Joseph (20/2/22).   (93)

(Shutterstock)

34. Binding, binding, binding!
(Promises)

'Jesus is the surety/ guarantee of the new covenant, because YHWH swore an oath that Jesus would be a high priest forever, after the order of Melchizedek....' (Hebrews 7 v 22).

The other night (24/1/22) I dreamt these words 'bind, bind, bind,' connected with seeking and finding, in my devotion: 'Keep on knocking...'
However, this sabbath evening (4/2/22) I read in our SDA Quarterly (2nd - 4th Feb' 22, p50-52) about the eternal priest, Jesus Christ, and how He's bound to us/ mankind, by this oath of Yahweh, in Hebrews. 7 v 22.

Melchizedek was a king of Salem and high priest, whom Abram met after defeating his enemies. The priest (mercifully) blessed Abram reminding him that it was Yahweh who had given him victory. In return Abram offered a tithe/ a tenth of his goods to the priest (and YHWH) (Gen. 14 v 18 - 20).

This oath differs from those given to earthly men, who will die, because it was given to someone who lives forever. Melchizedek has no recorded genealogy, no birth or death date, he's eternal (psalm 110 v 4; Hebs 7 v 1 - 3).
He is a type of Jesus, in that Jesus is eternal - He is First and Last, the Beginning and End, the Alpha and Omega, the Author and Finisher of our faith; He is the Word that was with YHWH at the Beginning of Creation (Isaiah 48 v 12 - 13; Rev. 1 v 4 & v 8; Rev. 22 v 13; & E G White, 'Steps to Christ', chp 8, p69; John 1 v 1 - 5).

Jesus is perfect, sinless and indestructible; He lives forever. So YHWH 's oath to make Him a High Priest, is binding forever. YHWH keeps His promises; so we can be certain of salvation through Jesus. ' YHWH binds Himself to humanity through His Son Jesus, Who though human, was pure, holy, sinless', ephemeral - **perfect**. 'Jesus binds humanity to divinity; heavenly family to the family of earth. Christ the high priest is our brother. Heaven is enshrined in humanity, and humanity is enfolded in the bosom of Infinite Love'.
(E G White, 'Desire of Ages', p25 -26).

PRAYER: Heavenly Father Yahweh, bless You, and thanks for Your bond of Love that keeps us closer yet to You, in perfect peace and harmony, through precious Jesus. Amen.   (95)   Doreen Joseph (4/2/22).

Tangerine flowers, London by Dors

(96)

35. Grace in Rejoicing
(Grace/ Encouragement)

'And not only so, but we glory in tribulations also: knowing that tribulation worketh patience; and patience, experience, and experience, hope: And hope maketh not ashamed; because the love of God is shed abroad in our hearts by the Holy Ghost which is given unto us'.
(Romans 5:3-5)

There are times when God's faithful members who have been living by His commandments truly have to face unpleasant situations, and these situations sometimes come one after another. During these testing times, members may begin to ask "has God abandoned me?" Many have questioned "have I done some wrong deed(s) that I have not confessed or ask God to forgive me for?" In these situations remember Job. He was God's faithful servant who went through so many trials, yet he continued to trust God.

It's just to help keep your mind in its right place; do not despair. See it as: these adversities are to prepare you for the spiritual battles you'll have to face, and they have come to make you strong and build your endurance.

Just gain the experience you need with each trial you have to face. Think deeply, think firmly, that God is preparing you for the things you have not seen, but will have to face. And all through He promises He'll never leave you.

Your battles are unique to you. As tribulation worketh patience, He'll support you through each and every one of your experiences.
He will not put you to shame. He will be there to support you.
Remain faithful. God's grace is sufficient to carry you through.

PRAYER:

Dear Father, help me to lean on you. You promise that Your grace is sufficient for me; that You will never leave me. I know and believe that
You are with me through all my trials.
Give me the courage to hold on to You whatever problem comes my way.
Amen.

Debbie Jones (Jan. '22).

(97)

Flowers in Kalifi, Kenya by Alithea

Advice / Admonition

Dor's roses, London

36. Guide Well Your Spirit
(Holiness)

Genesis 2:16 & 17 (KJV) And the Lord God commanded the man, saying, of every tree of the garden thou mayest freely eat. But of the tree of the knowledge of good and evil, thou shalt not eat of it, for in the day that thou eatest thereof thou shalt surely die.

Have you ever been privy to a conversation, read some form of literature, watched a movie or been in an environment where you have heard, read or seen things that felt disturbing to your spirit or so sinister that it prevented you from having a good nights' sleep? I believe we have all been there. My question is, 'is this within God's will?'

It was not God's will for Adam and Eve to know evil (White, E.G. (1930). This is still very much applicable for us today. The Bible tells us, "Whatsoever things are true, whatsoever things are honest, whatsoever things are just, whatsoever things are pure, whatsoever things are lovely, whatsoever things are of good report; if there be any virtue, and if there be any praise, think on these things" (Philippians 4:8).
Thus, we should guard well the avenues of the soul by refraining from reading, seeing, or hearing that which will derogate the mind and spirit from that which is holy (1 Peter 1:13 - 16).

The enemy is out to bring about our ruin. So let us therefore continuously pray to be guided by the Word of God and the Holy Spirit in all that we focus on, only then can we ensure that our spirit will be directed heavenwards (Psalm 119:11).

My Prayer – Kind Father in heaven, thank You for Your word and Your Holy Spirit to guide us in the path we ought to go. Help us to prayerfully resist the wiles of the tempter, and in so doing focus on that which will build our characters fit for Your kingdom. Thank You for Your patience with us. Help us to love You for You first loved us, in Jesus' name, I pray amen.

Ruth M. Chambers (May 2022)

(Shutterstock)

37. Focus On How God Sees You
(Godly focus)

1 Samuel 16:7 (KJV) But the Lord said unto Samuel, look not on his countenance, or on the height of his stature; because I have refused him: for the Lord seeth not as man seeth; for man looketh on the outward appearance, but the Lord looketh on the heart. Proverbs 14:12 (KJV) There is a way which seemeth right unto a man, but the end thereof are the ways of death.

It is detrimental to our spiritual growth and wellbeing to look to our fellow human beings for validation. Many in life have experienced discouragement and disappointment because we have chosen to focus on how people see us instead of how God sees us. God alone sees our heart, thus no one but God is qualified to judge us (James 4:12).

Self-focus is equally destructive. We are called to focus on God and to exalt God above all. The account of Peter walking on water (Matthew 14:28-31) is a profound revelation of what will be our fate if we turn our focus away from our Heavenly Father. Peter walked securely on water, however, in self-exaltation and in proudly seeking the admiration of his fellow disciples for the ease with which he trod upon water, Peter turned his eyes away from His Saviour, at that point Peter began to sink (White, E.G. (1898)).

Let us keep our focus upon the Lord of lords and King of kings, the only One who can save us.
God has not called us to focus on Him to forsake us or fail us.
To focus on God is happiness, joy, fulfillment and life.

My Prayer – Dear Heavenly Father, thank You that I only need to focus on You. Thank You that to focus on You is life. Help me to never turn my focus away from You, or to look to companions or even self, but to keep my eyes firmly fixed on You, so that I will live life abundantly.
I love You Father, thank You for being my everything,
in Jesus' name I pray, amen.

Ruth M. Chambers (July 2022)

Carol's red/ fuschia flowers, London

38. STOP! Don't lie; don't die...
(Admonition)

No entry to liars... (1 Corinthians 6 v 9 -11; Revelation 21 v 8)

Ladies, if tempted to sin with another woman's man, don't give
in! If tempted to cheat on your husband, don't do it!
It's not worth it.

'For liars, murderers, sorcerers/ magicians, fornicators/ promiscuous, sexually
immoral, homosexuals, abominable, cowards, idolaters, unbelievers, in short
LIARS, will not be permitted to enter heaven', nor have eternal life! (Rev. 21 v 8)

You wouldn't like to be treated that way;
Broken trust is hard to forgive. Broken hearts are hard to mend.
Emotional distress can be sickly and deadly.

So let's not go there. Be wise, and take good advice.
Life is too short to jeopardise your future.
Eternity beckons - offering a life of peace, joy, harmony, happiness and LOVE,
True love from our heavenly Father Yahweh and Jesus Christ.

They already proved Their love for you, when Jesus died on Calvary's cross.
Don't turn a blind eye; or be an ungrateful swine (Matthew 7 v 6).

Love Yahweh, love Christ,
Love Their kind of life,

And live forever, happy and free. Selah.

PRAYER:

Holy Spirit, help us to turn away from temptation, to not succumb, but
instead overcome, and be victorious with
Christ Jesus, our precious Lord and King. Amen.

Doreen Joseph (24/1/22).

(Shutterstock)

YHWH's grace and love is 'exceedingly abundant' for us,

(Ephesians 3 v 20 - 21)

(106)

39. Keep on knocking..and He will open the door
(Advice)

**BIND! BIND! BIND!! Keep seeking, you will find (YHWH),
(1 Chronicles 28 v 9; 2 Chronicles 15 v 2; Jeremiah 29 v 13).
Persist in asking, you will find your design. 'Ask, and it shall be given you;
seek, and you shall find; knock, and it shall be opened unto you; for every
one who asks, receives... (Matt. 7 v 7 - 8). Ask Father for what you want,
and He will give you your needs (Matt 6 v 25 -34; Philippians 4 v 19); even
He'll give you your heart's desires, if you delight yourself in Jehovah,
(Psalm 37 v 4).**

Hannah persevered in praying for a child for many years barren; then prophet
Eli overheard her anguished (not drunken) prayers at the temple one day.
She had vowed to dedicate her child to the Lord, if He would grant her
petition. Eli reassured her that Yahweh had granted her desire. And indeed
she bore a son, named Samuel. And when he was weaned, she kept her vow,
and brought him, and dedicated him, to serve the Lord at the temple.
The child became a great prophet of Jehovah. (1 Samuel 1 v 9 - 28).

Jesus told the story of the importunate widow, who persistently begged an
unjust judge to avenge her adversaries. And he, who cared less about man or
Jehovah, was forced to give in lest she torment him. How much more will our
heavenly Father Yahweh answer our petitions if we are persistent,
(Luke 18 v 1 - 8); and pray without ceasing, (1 Thessalonians 5 v 16 - 18)?

Indeed, how much more is YHWH willing to give us the Holy Spirit, than evil
parents/ sinners give good gifts to their children, (Luke 11 v 13)? Ellen G White
wrote 'we do not have much because we do not ask great things of Yahweh.
He doesn't do mediocre. He does MIRACLES!!! ('Steps to Christ' chp 11).
Let's not be shy or precious, unwilling to trouble the Lord with our requests.
Be bold and speak aloud our petitions, and He will surely hear from heaven,
and answer.

PRAISES:

Hallelujah, amen. Thank you, Father Yahweh, for letting Jesus open the veil/
door via death on Calvary's cross, to enable us to come boldly before Your
throne and make known our petitions. We have the assurance / confidence
that if we ask anything in Your Son, Jesus' name, that You will grant it,
(1 John 5 v 14). Hallelujah, amen.   (107)   Doreen Joseph (24/1/22)

Special prayers

THE AUTHOR DOREEN JOSEPH IS WEST LONDONER, AND POSTGRADU-ATE OF BRUNEL AND LONDON UNIVERSI-TIES, IN SOCIAL SCEIENCES. SHE HAS BEEN A TEACHER, RESEARCHER, MENTAL HEALTH ADVOCATE, AND LECTURER. HER MAIN PRE-OCCUPATION IS WRITING, WITH RECENT PUB-LICATION OF 'PERFECT CIRCLES   VOL 1 - AN EXPLORATION OF FAITH & RELATIONSHIPS WITH YHWH (YAHWEH) - OUR HEAVENLY FATHER. THIS NEW BOOK HAS CHILD CONTRIBUTORS, HER GRAND-SONS MATISSE AND DILLON.   FRIEND JAYNIELIA, AND GROWN UPS GOOD FRIEND DELORES;   AND TEENAGE DAUGHTER SAFRON,   AND ILLUSTRATOR JANINE, BOTH UNIVERSITY STUDENTS.

  'PRAYERS FOR A CHILD' IS FOR ANY CHILD (OR GROWN UP) WHO FEELS THE NEED TO REACH OUT FOR HELP TO SOMEONE WHO WILL ALWAYS LISTEN, OUR CREATOR.   SOMETIMES WE ARE IN DIFFICULT SITU-ATIONS, AND PRAYER OFFERS SOME COMFORT, AND SOLUTIONS TO OUR PROBLEMS. OTHER TIMES WE PRAISE AND THANK OUR MAKER FOR HIS BLESSINGS AND SAVING US, AS WE LEARN TO LOVE HIM IN RETURN. AND WE PRAY FOR OUR LOVED ONES, AND OTHERS IN THE WORLD.   THROUGH PRAYER WE TALK TO   OUR CREATOR AND HE 'IS WELL PLEASED'. FOR JESUS CHRIST SAID ' SUFFER THE LITTLE CHILDREN TO COME UNTO ME'..

Barcode Area

We will add the barcode for you.

Made with Cover Creator

PRAYERS FOR A CHILD

DOREEN JOSEPH & CONTRIBUTORS

ILLUSTRATOR JANINE HARVEY

40. Pray for our youths
(Advice)

'Seek and dedicate yourself to the Lord whilst you are still young, before the cares of the world distract you.' (Ecclesiastes 12 v 1).

As parents, grandparents and responsible adults we are very concerned about our children and young people, who are daily exposed to increasing dangers - morally, emotionally, physically, mentally and spiritually.

How often do we hear of very young children self-harming, or even committing suicide? How much are they terrorised by bullying physically, mentally, or virtually through social media? Peer pressures, exam worries, materialism, decline in moral standards, beleaguer them; and there's a lack of firm foundations to guide them how to live good, safe, upstanding lives, with compassion and consideration for others.

Help us point the youngsters to that sure foundation, the 'Word' that is Jesus Christ, and His Bible. And let not only our words, but our actions - our lives, show good principles and practices.

E. G. White wrote in 'Messages to Young People': ' O, that young men might appreciate the high destiny to which they are called! ....Young men (and women) who give themselves wholly to (YHWH), who are uncorrupted by vice and impurity, would be ennobled to do great work for (Yahweh). Let young men (and women) heed admonition and be sober-minded.' (p.22)

. Yes, if only they would 'dedicate themselves to the Lord in their youth,' how much more profitable and happy would their lives be.

PRAYER:

Please pray along with us for heavenly Father Yahweh to guide and protect all our children and young people.
May Yahweh surround them with holy angels, in 'gentle' and loving Jesus name, we pray, amen.

Doreen Joseph (3/1/22).

Photoshot by Mercedes

(112)

Epilogue

The ultimate feast & celebration: the
'Marriage feast of the Lamb, our Lord Creator, REDEEMER, and Saviour,
dearest JESUS CHRIST,
wedded to His 'bride' - the 'elect' people of all races and nations,
Whom He saves from the fire and brimstone of the second, and permanent
death, namely, permanent *separation* from Holy Heavenly Father YHWH.
(Rev. 7 v 10; Rev. 19 v 6 - 9; Rev. 21 v 21; Roms. 8 v 33; Rev. 7; Rev. 20 v 10 & 21 v 8)

Halleluiahs! Rejoice, evermore, galore!

(Doreen's, DJKO, painting, 2014/2015, on front cover of Perfect Circles vol. 3)

(114)

Song: Give your thanks to the Lord...
(Thanksgiving)

On the 5th Feb. '22, at 5.15 am I was just dozing off back to sleep, before the 5.20 alarm for church Prayer Line, when I dreamt the following:

I was leading a group of 10 - 15 Black women who were writing together their devotions to the Lord. We were happy, joyful in the endeavour. We rubbed/ anointed our arms with perfumed lotions, and were eating celebratory food. We were just simply enjoying being united in this project - writing a book of devotions; and we sang a joyful song:-

"Give your thanks to the Lord, All the earth, let us sing! All the earth give your thanks , Let us sing!

Again: "Give your thanks and praises to the Lord!"

Our joyful, loud singing sounded like a black gospel choir, soulful, melodious, rich and heavenly!   Marvellous!!!

We were singing our hearts out; lungs full blast, with happiness and joy! Happy to have this privilege of knowing and loving the Lord, and encouraging each other, and others.

Listen!   Halleluiahs and amens galore!!!

I am grateful to the ladies, church sisters and friends, writers - Ruth, Debbie, Lucy and Sharon; and Carol and my daughters Safron and Alithea - photographers, and Ruth's daughter Mercedes - photoshot expert, for agreeing to go on this journey with me to produce this compilation of devotions and images.

I know they are represented in my dream, even a premonition, of the great celebration we have ahead of us - after the completion of our book; *and* of the future celebration of the 'marriage feast of the Lamb, Jesus Christ, (Rev. 19 v 6-9) of Whom we hope and pray we will be His honoured, invited guests.

PRAISES: Meantime, **Give thanks to the Lord, all the earth. Let us sing!**

Doreen Joseph (5 & 20/2/22).

(115)

(authors in horseshoe formation:- Doreen, Ruth, Debbie, Lucy, Sharon)
Photoshot by Mercedes

Printed in Great Britain
by Amazon

21890338R00077